BIOGRAPHIES

Thomas Jefferson

A Founding Father of the United States of America

by LORI MORTENSEN   illustrated by LEN EBERT

PICTURE WINDOW BOOKS
Minneapolis, Minnesota

Special thanks to our advisers for their expertise:

Robin H. Gabriel, Hunter J. Smith Director of Education
Monticello/Thomas Jefferson Foundation
Charlottesville, Virginia

Terry Flaherty, Ph.D., Professor of English
Minnesota State University, Mankato

Editor: Jill Kalz
Designer: Hilary Wacholz
Page Production: Michelle Biedscheid
Art Director: Nathan Gassman
Associate Managing Editor: Christianne Jones
The illustrations in this book were created with color inks and color pencils.
Photo Credit: Library of Congress, page 3

Picture Window Books
5115 Excelsior Boulevard, Suite 232
Minneapolis, MN 55416
877-845-8392
www.picturewindowbooks.com

Printed in the United States of America.

Library of Congress Cataloging-in-Publication Data
Mortensen, Lori, 1955–
Thomas Jefferson, a founding father of the United States of America / by Lori
Mortensen; illustrated by Len Ebert.
p. cm. — (Biographies)
Includes index.
ISBN 978-1-4048-3729-4 (library binding)
1. Jefferson, Thomas, 1743–1826—Juvenile literature. 2. Presidents—United States—
Biography—Juvenile literature. 3. Founding Fathers of the United States—Biography—
Juvenile literature. 4. United States. Declaration of Independence—Juvenile literature.
5. United States—Politics and government—1775–1783—Juvenile literature. I. Ebert,
Len. II. Title.
E332.79.M59 2008
973.4'6092—dc22   2007032892

Thomas Jefferson was one of the most important leaders in U.S. history. His ideas about freedom shaped the country's government. He wrote the Declaration of Independence. He later served as vice president and as third president of the United States.

This is the story of
Thomas Jefferson.

Thomas Jefferson was born in Virginia on April 13, 1743. His family lived on a large farm called a plantation. Many slaves worked in his family's tobacco fields.

Thomas loved to learn. He knew how to read and write by the time he was 5 years old. Later, he studied Greek, French, and Latin. He also played the violin.

Thomas was not good at speaking in front of others.
He often put his thoughts down on paper instead of
saying them aloud.

When Thomas was 14, his father died. At first, Thomas felt lost. But he kept at his studies. When he was 17, he went to college and became a lawyer.

Eight years later, in 1768, he was elected to the Virginia Legislature. He helped make laws for people in the Virginia Colony.

Thomas had other dreams, too. In 1768, he began clearing land for his own home on a mountaintop. He called it Monticello, the Italian word for "little mountain."

Soon Thomas met Martha Wayles Skelton. She loved books and music as much as he did. In 1772, the couple married on New Year's Day. Their first child, a girl named Martha, was born nine months later. The couple would have five more children together.

Thomas and Martha were very happy. But many of their fellow American colonists were not.

At that time, the Colonies were still ruled by the king of Britain. The king was in favor of laws the Colonists did not like. Some people believed Americans should fight for freedom. Others believed they should stay loyal to the king.

Thomas believed people should be able to choose their own leaders and make their own laws. In 1774, he wrote a paper about these ideas. It was called "A Summary View of the Rights of British America." Not everyone agreed with Thomas' ideas. But everyone did agree that Thomas was a talented writer.

The following year, in 1775, the Colonists began fighting for their freedom. Their fight against the British king was called the Revolutionary War (1775–1783).

Thomas and other leaders gathered in Philadelphia, Pennsylvania, for a special meeting. Together, they formed the Continental Congress. They wanted to tell everyone about America's independence from Britain. The other leaders asked Thomas to write the Declaration of Independence.

Thomas, now 33 years old, worked on the paper for 17 days. He wrote some of the most powerful words ever written. The Declaration of Independence said that the Colonies were breaking away from Britain. It said that all people were created equal. It said that everyone had certain freedoms and rights.

When Thomas finished, he showed the paper to the other leaders. They wanted to make some changes. The men argued for three days. Finally, on July 4, 1776, everyone agreed.

The United States of America was born.

After leaving the Continental Congress in the fall of 1776, Thomas served in the Virginia Legislature. In 1779, he was elected governor.

In 1789, George Washington became the first president of the United States. He asked Thomas to be his secretary of state. Thomas agreed. This put Thomas in charge of the United States' relationships with other countries.

When John Adams became president in 1797, Thomas became vice president. Four years later, Thomas became the third president of the United States. He was 57 years old.

Thomas served as president for eight years. He did many things for the country, including lowering taxes. He also purchased the Louisiana Territory, which doubled the size of the United States. He asked Meriwether Lewis and William Clark to explore the new land.

At the end of his term, Thomas moved back to Monticello. But he did not stop working. He helped create the University of Virginia. He believed his work for better education was more important than being president of the United States.

Thomas Jefferson died at Monticello on July 4, 1826, the 50th anniversary of the Declaration of Independence.

The Life of Thomas Jefferson

1743	Born at Shadwel a, on April 13
1768	Elected to Virginia Legislature
1772	Married Martha Wayles Skelton
1774	Wrote a paper called "A Summary View of the Rights of British America"
1776	Wrote the Declaration of Independence
1779	Served as governor of Virginia
1782	Martha died after giving birth to the couple's sixth child
1784	Became minister to France
1790	Became secretary of state
1797	Became John Adams' vice president
1801	Became third president of the United States
1817	Began creating the University of Virginia
1826	Died at Monticello on July 4, at age 83

Did You Know?

~ Thomas was the third of 10 children. He grew to be 6 feet 3 inches (189 centimeters) tall.

~ Thomas had many talents. He studied art, math, and science. He invented many things. He could read in seven languages: English, French, Spanish, Italian, Latin, Greek, and Anglo-Saxon.

~ Thomas and Martha had six children together. Only two of their children survived to become adults.

~ In 1784, Thomas replaced Benjamin Franklin as the U.S. minister to France. During his five years in Paris, Thomas worked toward signing business treaties (agreements) with other countries.

Glossary

colony — an area of land ruled by another country; people who live in a colony are called colonists

Continental Congress — a group of people from the American Colonies that managed the United States government during the Revolutionary War

independence — freedom from the control of other people or another government

lawyer — a person who has studied law (the rules of a community, state, or nation) and can give advice

legislature — a group of people with the power to make laws for a state or nation

slaves — a person who is owned by another person

taxes — money that people must give to the government to pay for what the government does

To Learn More

More Books to Read

Kishel, Ann-Marie. *Thomas Jefferson: A Life of Patriotism.* Minneapolis: Lerner Publications, 2006.

Raatma, Lucia. *Thomas Jefferson.* Minneapolis: Compass Point Books, 2001.

Ribke, Simone T. *Thomas Jefferson.* New York: Children's Press, 2003.

Sirimarco, Elizabeth. *Thomas Jefferson: Our Third President.* Chanhassen, Minn.: Child's World, 2002.

On the Web

FactHound offers a safe, fun way to find Web sites related to topics in this book. All of the sites on FactHound have been researched by our staff.

1. Visit *www.facthound.com*

2. Type in this special code: 1404837299

3. Click on the FETCH IT button.

Your trusty FactHound will fetch the best sites for you!

Index

Look for all of the books in the Biographies series:

Abraham Lincoln: *Lawyer, President, Emancipator*

Albert Einstein: *Scientist and Genius*

Amelia Earhart: *Female Pioneer in Flight*

Benjamin Franklin: *Writer, Inventor, Statesman*

Booker T. Washington: *Teacher, Speaker, and Leader*

Cesar Chavez: *Champion and Voice of Farmworkers*

Frederick Douglass: *Writer, Speaker, and Opponent of Slavery*

George Washington: *Farmer, Soldier, President*

George Washington Carver: *Teacher, Scientist, and Inventor*

Harriet Tubman: *Hero of the Underground Railroad*

Jackie Robinson: *Hero and Athlete*

Marie Curie: *Prize-Winning Scientist*

Martha Washington: *First Lady of the United States*

Martin Luther King Jr.: *Preacher, Freedom Fighter, Peacemaker*

Pocahontas: *Peacemaker and Friend to the Colonists*

Sally Ride: *Astronaut, Scientist, Teacher*

Sojourner Truth: *Preacher for Freedom and Equality*

Susan B. Anthony: *Fighter for Freedom and Equality*

Thomas Edison: *Inventor, Scientist, and Genius*

Thomas Jefferson: *A Founding Father of the United States of America*